The BIG RHODE ISLAND REPRODUCIBLE Activity Book!

BY CAROLE MARSH

This activity book has material which correlates with the Rhode Island Framework for Social Studies.

At every opportunity, we have tried to relate information to the Rhode Island History and Social Science, English, Science, Math, Civics, Economics, and Computer Technology directives.

For additional information, go to our websites:
www.rhodeislandexperience.com or **www.gallopade.com**.

The Big Activity Book Team

Billie Walburn
Michael Marsh
Antoinette Miller
Michele Yother
Carole Marsh
Steven Saint-Laurent
Bob Longmeyer
Kathy Zimmer
Chad Beard
Pam Dufresne
Cranston Davenport
Al Fortunatti
Victoria DeJoy
Terry Briggs
Jackie Clayton
Pat Newman
Cecil Anderson
Sherry Moss
Shery Kearney

Permission is hereby granted to the individual purchaser or classroom teacher to reproduce materials in this book for non-commercial individual or classroom use only.

Reproduction of these materials for an entire school or school system is strictly prohibited.

Gallopade is proud to be a member of these educational organizations and associations:

Published by
GALLOPADE INTERNATIONAL
800-536-2GET
www.gallopade.com

The Rhode Island Experience Series

My First Pocket Guide to Rhode Island!

The Rhode Island Coloring Book!

My First Book About Rhode Island!

Rhode Island Jeopardy: Answers and Questions About Our State

Rhode Island "Jography!": A Fun Run Through Our State

The Rhode Island Experience! Sticker Pack

The Rhode Island Experience! Poster/Map

Discover Rhode Island CD-ROM

Rhode Island "GEO" Bingo Game

Rhode Island "HISTO" Bingo Game

A Word From The Author

Rhode Island is a very special state. Almost everything about Rhode Island is interesting and fun! It has a remarkable history that helped create the great nation of America. Rhode Island enjoys an amazing geography of incredible beauty and fascination. The state's people are unique and have accomplished many great things.

This Activity Book is chock-full of activities to entice you to learn more about Rhode Island. While completing puzzles, coloring activities, word codes, and other fun-to-do activities, you'll learn about your state's history, geography, people, places, animals, legends, and more.

Whether you're sitting in a classroom, stuck inside on a rainy day, or–better yet–sitting in the back seat of a car touring the wonderful state of Rhode Island, my hope is that you have as much fun using this Activity Book as I did writing it.

Enjoy your Rhode Island Experience–it's the trip of a lifetime!!

Carole Marsh

Geographic Tools

Beside each geographic need listed, put the initials of the tool that can best help you!

(CR) Compass Rose (LL) Longitude and Latitude
(M) Map (G) Grid
(K) Map key/legend

1. ____ I need to find the geographic location of Germany.

2. ____ I need to learn where an airport is located near Providence.

3. ____ I need to find which way is north.

4. ____ I need to chart a route from Rhode Island to California.

5. ____ I need to find a small town on a map.

Match the items on the left with the items on the right.

1. Grid system
2. Compass rose
3. Longitude and latitude
4. Two of Rhode Island's borders
5. Symbols on a map

A. Map key or legend
B. Massachusetts and Connecticut
C. A system of letters and numbers
D. Imaginary lines around the earth
E. Shows N, S, E, and W

ANSWERS: 1-LL; 2-K; 3-CR; 4-M; 5-G; 1-C; 2-E; 3-D; 4-B; 5-A

©2001 Carole Marsh/Gallopade International/800-536-2GET/www.rhodeislandexperience.com/Page 5

Rhode Island's First Settlers!

Read the paragraph below, then answer the following questions.

Roger Williams settled in Providence around 1636, near a freshwater spring. He named the place "Providence" and declared it as a haven for people seeking religious freedom. Three other settlements followed, and in 1644, Williams obtained a charter from the English Parliament for the "Providence Plantations in Narragansett Bay." For a long time, the government of Rhode Island shifted between two capitals, Newport and Providence. In 1900, Providence became the official capital.

1. _____ settled in Providence around 1636, near a freshwater spring.

2. Roger Williams named _____ and declared it a haven for people seeking religious freedom.

3. For a time, Rhode Island shifted its government between two capital cities: _____ and _____.

4. In _____ Williams obtained a charter from the English Parliament for the "Providence Plantations in Narragansett Bay."

5. The present-day capital of Rhode Island is _____, which became the capital in _____.

ANSWERS: 1-Roger Williams; 2-Providence; 3-Newport and Providence; 4-1644; 5-Providence, 1900

Rhode Island Government!

Rhode Island's state government, just like our national government, is made up of three branches. Each branch has a certain job to do. Each branch also has some power over the other branches. We call this system checks and balances. The three branches work together to make our government work smoothly.

Legislative Branch

This branch is made up of two houses, the Senate and the House of Representatives. It is also called the General Assembly. The members of this branch make and repeal laws.

Executive Branch

The governor heads the executive branch which includes the lieutenant governor, attorney general, secretary of state, general treasurer, and eight directors of state departments.

Judicial Branch

The court system is included in this branch. Local, district, and state courts are part of the judicial system which interprets the laws.

For each of these government officials, circle whether they are part of the EXECUTIVE, the LEGISLATIVE, or the JUDICIAL branch.

1. the governor	EXECUTIVE LEGISLATIVE JUDICIAL	
2. a state representative	EXECUTIVE LEGISLATIVE JUDICIAL	
3. a state senator	EXECUTIVE LEGISLATIVE JUDICIAL	
4. secretary of state	EXECUTIVE LEGISLATIVE JUDICIAL	
5. chief justice of the State Supreme Court	EXECUTIVE LEGISLATIVE JUDICIAL	
6. speaker of the House of Representatives	EXECUTIVE LEGISLATIVE JUDICIAL	
7. general treasurer	EXECUTIVE LEGISLATIVE JUDICIAL	
8. district court judge	EXECUTIVE LEGISLATIVE JUDICIAL	
9. attorney general	EXECUTIVE LEGISLATIVE JUDICIAL	
10. a member of the General Assembly	EXECUTIVE LEGISLATIVE JUDICIAL	

The number of legislators may change after each census.

ANSWERS: 1-executive; 2-legislative; 3-legislative; 4-executive; 5-judicial; 6-legislative; 7-executive; 8-judicial; 9-executive; 10-legislative

All Around Rhode Island Bubblegram

Fill in the bubblegram by using the clues below.

1. Rhode Island's state capital
2. Coastal town founded by Samuel Gorton
3. Southwest of Providence; has third-largest state population
4. Site of Slater Mill; located northeast of Providence
5. South of Tiverton, the town where the Rhode Island Red rooster was bred.

1. _ _ O _ _ _ O _ O _

2. _ O _ _ _ _ _

3. _ _ _ O O _ _ _

4. _ O _ O _ _ O _

5. _ _ _ _ _ _ _ _ _ O _ _

Now unscramble the "bubble" letters to find out the mystery words!

HINT: Rhode Island's nickname

The _ _ _ _ _ _ _ _ _ _

ANSWERS: 1-Providence; 2-Warwick; 3-Cranston; 4-Pawtucket; 5 Little Compton
MYSTERY WORDS: Ocean State

Rhode Island Rebus!

Known as the Ocean State, Rhode Island has a wealth of salt ponds and marshes. Separated from the Atlantic Ocean by barrier beaches, the coastal lagoons or salt ponds are home to a variety of fish, shrimp, and birds including egrets, herons and kingfishers. The lagoons are shallow, which allows eelgrass to grow and fill the area. Insects eat the grass, and fish and shellfish feed on algae. At low tide, saltwater pools form around the rocks, serving as natural aquariums for small fish, crabs, snails, and barnacles. The saltmarshes are wetlands that provide a banquet of natural foods for small sea creatures and mammals. Tall grasses and boggy soil are typically found in the saltmarshes.

What kind of creatures can you find in the saltmarsh? Solve the puzzles below for the answers?

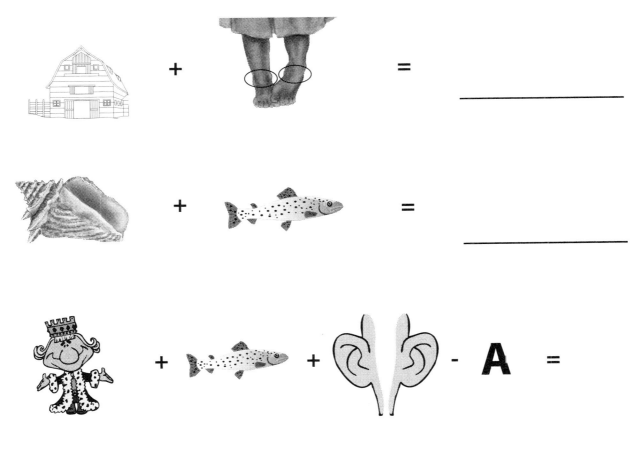

ANSWERS: 1-barracles; 2-shellfish; 3-kingfishers

Rhode Island Wheel of Fortune, Indian Style!

The names of Rhode Island's many Native American tribes contain enough consonants to play....Wheel of Fortune!

See if you can figure out the Wheel of Fortune-style puzzles below! "Vanna" has given you some of the consonants in each word.

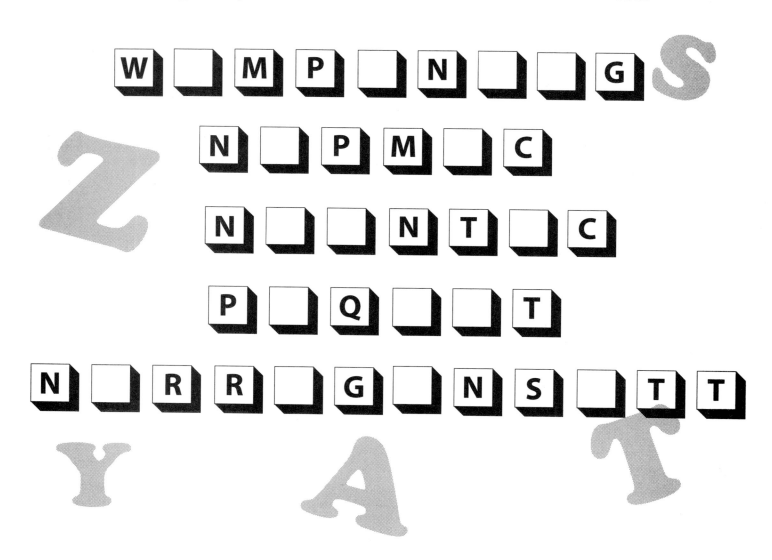

ANSWERS: Wampanoag; Nipmuc; Niantic; Pequot; Narragansett

©2001 Carole Marsh/Gallopade International/800-536-2GET/www.rhodeislandexperience.com/Page 10

Rainbow, Pretty Rainbow

Rainbows often appear over Block Island after a storm. Rainbows are formed when sunlight bends through raindrops. Big raindrops produce the brightest, most beautiful rainbows. You can see rainbows early or late on a rainy day when the sun is behind you.

Color the rainbow in the order the colors are listed below, starting at the top of the rainbow. Then, in each band write down as many Rhode Island-related words as you can think of that begin with the same first letter as that color!

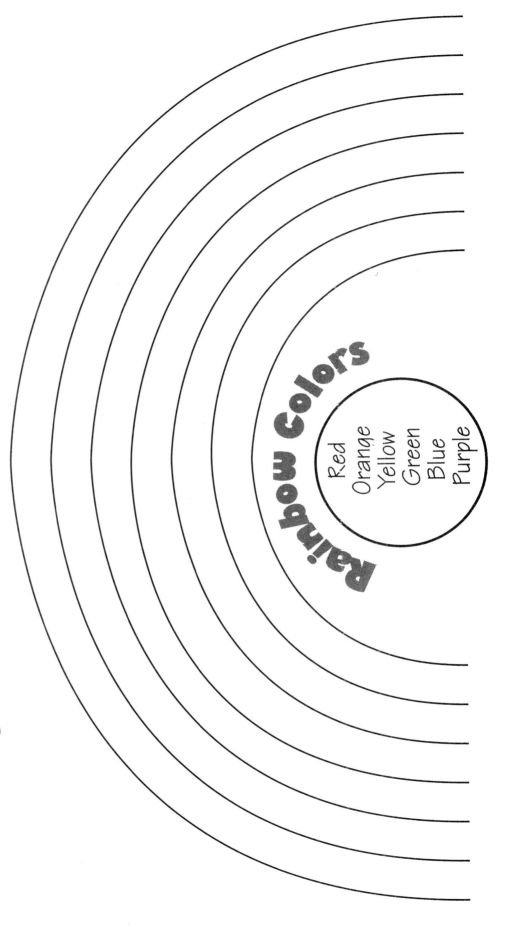

Rainbow Colors
- Red
- Orange
- Yellow
- Green
- Blue
- Purple

©2001 Carole Marsh/Gallopade International/800-536-2GET/www.rhodeislandexperience.com/Page 11

In the Beginning... Came the Europeans!

One of the first explorers to discover present day Narragansett Bay was Giovanni da Verrazzano in 1524. He was an Italian explorer who was excited about the land and riches available in the New World. Roger Williams, an Englishman seeking religious freedom from the restrictions he faced in nearby Boston, Massachusetts, founded Providence.

Help Verrazzano sail into Narragansett Bay!

🔖 Sam Gorton founded the city of Warwick.

🔖 Ann and William Hutchinson came to Rhode Island in search of religious expression and founded Portsmouth.

©2001 Carole Marsh/Gallopade International/800-536-2GET/www.rhodeislandexperience.com/Page 12

U.S. Time Zones

Would you believe that the contiguous United States is divided into four time zones? It is! Because of the rotation of the earth, the sun travels from east to west. Whenever the sun is directly overhead, we call that time noon. When it is noon in Rhode Island, the sun has a long way to go before it is directly over San Francisco, California. When it is 12:00 p.m. (noon) in Providence, it is 11:00 a.m. in Chicago, Illinois. There is a one-hour time difference between each zone!

Look at the time zones on the map below, then answer the following questions:

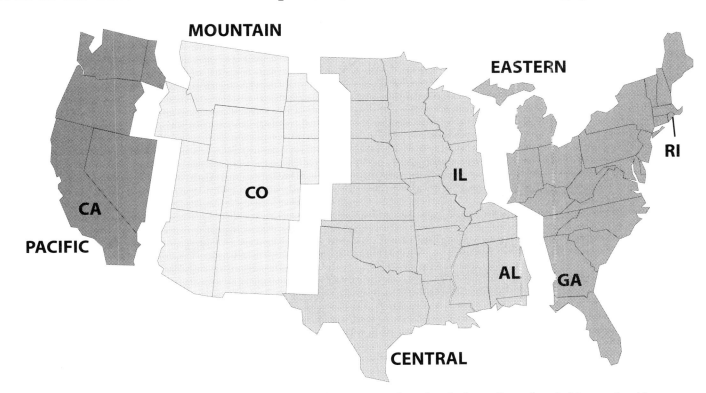

1. When it is 10:00 a.m. in Providence, Rhode Island, what time is it in California? _____ a.m.

2. When it is 3:30 p.m. in Atlanta, Georgia, what time is it in Rhode Island? _____ p.m.

3. In what time zone is Rhode Island located? _____

4. In what time zone is Colorado located? _____

5. If it is 10:00 p.m. in Scituate, Rhode Island, what time is it in Alabama? _____ p.m.

ANSWERS: 1-7:00 a.m.; 2-3:30 p.m.; 3-Eastern; 4-Mountain; 5-9:00 p.m.

Sing Like a Rhode Island Bird Word Jumble!

Arrange the jumbled letters in the proper order for the names of birds found in Rhode Island.

1. C K D U _ _ _ _
2. L G U L _ _ _ _
3. N R H O E _ _ _ _ _
4. A I R L _ _ _ _
5. S O O G E _ _ _ _ _
6. A N T C O R M O R _ _ _ _ _ _ _ _ _
7. T N E R _ _ _ _
8. T C A B R D I _ _ _ _ _ _ _
9. A W B R E L R _ _ _ _ _ _ _
10. S P O R Y E _ _ _ _ _ _

Catbird   Cormorant   Duck   Goose   Gull   Heron   Osprey   Rail   Tern   Warbler

ANSWERS: 1-Duck; 2-Gull; 3-Heron; 4-Rail; 5-Goose; 6-Cormorant; 7-Tern; 8-Catbird; 9-Warbler; 10-Osprey

©2001 Carole Marsh/Gallopade International/800-536-2GET/www.rhodeislandexperience.com/Page 14

Rhode Island Schools Rule!

The first Rhode Island university was chartered in Warren as Rhode Island College in 1764, moved to Providence in 1770, and renamed Brown University in 1804. Other Rhode Island colleges and universities include the Rhode Island School of Design and Johnson and Wales University, both in Providence. Salve Regina University is located in Newport, and the University of Rhode Island has its main campus in Kingston. The U.S. Naval War College was founded in Newport in 1885 and focuses on postgraduate training for officers in the armed forces of the United States and its allies.

Complete the names of these Rhode Island schools. Use the Word Bank to help you. Then, use the answers to solve the code at the bottom.

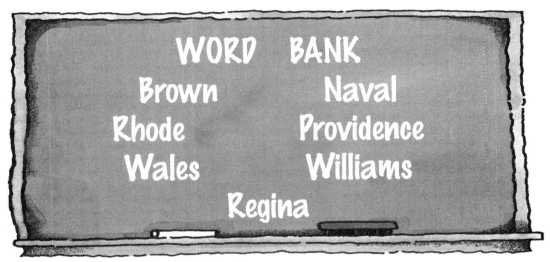

1. U.S. _ _ _ _ _ War College

2. Johnson and _ _ _ _ _ University

3. _ _ _ _ _ Island College in _ _ _ _ _ _ _ _ _ _
          1   3

4. _ _ _ _ _ University
           5

5. Roger _ _ _ _ _ _ _ _ College
            2   4   6

6. Salve _ _ _ _ _ _ University
                 7

The coded message tells you what all college students want!

_ _ _ _ _ _ _
1 2 3 4 5 6 7

ANSWERS: 1-Naval; 2-Wales; 3-Rhode, Providence; 4-Brown; 5-Williams; 6-Regina
MESSAGE: diploma

©2001 Carole Marsh/Gallopade International/800-536-2GET/www.rhodeislandexperience.com/Page 15

Rhode Island Topography is "Tops"!

When we learn about Rhode Island's topography, we use special words to describe it. These words describe the things that make each part of the state interesting.

Cross out every other letter below beginning with the first one to find out what each topographical term is!

1. K I H S G L X A Y N P D
    a body of land surrounded by water

2. N B S A K Y
    a body of water partially surrounded by land

3. T R O I B V W E M R
    a large natural stream of flowing water

4. T V O A P L P L T E D Y
    an elongated natural depression in the earth bordered by higher land

5. F P H E C N X I G N K S W U E L Z A
    a piece of land surrounded on three sides by water

6. Y H A I P L D L
    land that rises above its surroundings and has a rounded summit

ANSWERS: 1-island; 2-bay; 3-river; 4-valley; 5-peninsula; 6-hill

Oh! Say Can You See...
The Rhode Island State Flag

Rhode Island's current state flag was adopted in 1897. It features a white background with a golden anchor in the center. The anchor dates back to 1647, when Rhode Island and the Providence Plantations were established under King Charles II of England. The colors blue and white were flown during the American Revolution, War of 1812, and Mexican-American War. A blue ribbon underneath bears the word "HOPE." Thirteen gold stars encircle the anchor and the ribbon.

Color the Rhode Island flag.

Design your own Diamante on Rhode Island!

A *diamante* is a cool diamond-shaped poem on any subject.

You can write your very own diamante poem on Rhode Island by following the simple line by line directions below. Give it a try!

Line 1: Write the name of Rhode Island's capital

Line 2: Write Rhode Island's nickname

Line 3: Write the names of three Rhode Island Native American tribes

Line 4: Write the names of four Rhode Island rivers

Line 5: Write the names of the state flower, state mineral, and state shell

Line 6: Write the name of Rhode Island's state tree

Line 7: Write the state motto

_____

_____   _____

_____   _____   _____

_____   _____   _____   _____

_____   _____   _____

_____   _____

_____

YOU'RE a poet! Did you know it?

History Mystery Tour!

Rhode Island is bursting at the seams with history! Here are just a few of the many historical sites that you might visit. Try your hand at locating them on the map!

Draw the symbol for each site on the Rhode Island map below.

 The Armory of the Artillery Company of Newport was built in the mid-1830s. It houses a large collection of weapons and military items.

 The name **Pawtucket** means "place by the waterfall." This city was once an early industrial center.

 Joseph Brown House, located in Providence, was designed by Brown in 1774. It is described as a whimsical house with a curving gable and original doorway on the second floor.

 Fort Ningret State Historic Site in Charlestown is the site of the original outline of a Dutch fort which predates the Pilgrims' Plymouth landing in 1620.

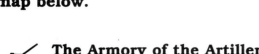 **Jamestown, on Conanicut Island**, was settled by Quakers. A windmill stands in the center of the island.

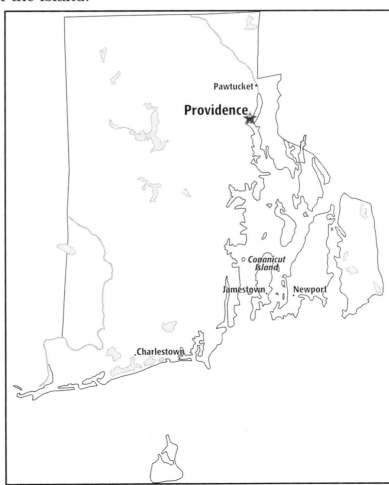

What in the World?

A hemisphere is one-half of a sphere (globe) created by the prime meridian or equator. Every place in the world is in two hemispheres (Northern or Southern and Eastern or Western). The equator is an imaginary line that runs around the world from left to right and divides the globe into the Northern Hemisphere and the Southern Hemisphere. The prime meridian is an imaginary line that runs around the world from top to bottom and divides the globe into the Eastern Hemisphere and Western Hemisphere.

Label the Northern and Southern Hemispheres.

Write E on the equator.

Is Rhode Island in the NORTHERN or SOUTHERN Hemisphere? (circle one)

Color the map.

Label the Eastern and Western Hemispheres.

Write PM on the prime meridian.

Is Rhode Island in the EASTERN or WESTERN Hemisphere? (circle one)

Color the map.

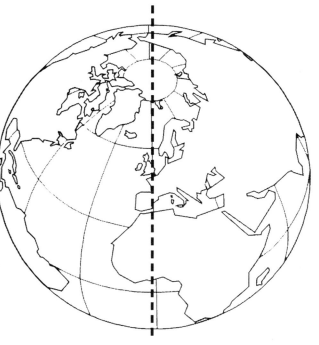

ANSWERS: Northern; Western

Places to Go! Things to Do!

Rhode Island has so many cool places to go and so many cool things to do! Pack your bags for a whirlwind tour of Rhode Island's most historic sites!

Use the Word Bank to help you complete the sentences below and learn about some of the exciting Rhode Island sites you can visit!

WORD BANK
Brick School House
Gothic Castle
Moffatt Mill
Providence Arcade
Slater Mill

1. The _____ is one of the first school buildings in the city; now headquarters of the Providence Preservation Society.

2. The old state arsenal in Providence was designed by Russell Warren and built in 1839. It is called _____.

3. Go shopping at the _____, the nation's first enclosed shopping mall, built in 1828 in Greek Revival style.

4. _____ in Pawtucket was the first textile mill in the country powered by water.

5. _____ in Lincoln is a small water-powered factory.

ANSWERS: 1-Brick School House; 2-Gothic Castle; 3-Providence Arcade; 4-Slater Mill; 5-Moffatt Mill

Please Come to Rhode Island!

You have a friend who lives in Georgia. She is thinking of moving to Rhode Island because she wants to be a preservationist. A preservationist is a person who works to keep buildings or items from being destroyed, especially things of historical significance. Rhode Island is in the process of preserving and restoring many of its historic buildings and homes. It's a place that's rich in history and culture.

Write her a letter describing Rhode Island and some of the preservationist opportunities there.

Newport is a great place for preservationists. The Preservation Society of Newport County has saved many structures including the Hunter House, its first acquisition. The house is filled with furniture made by early American cabinetmakers. There are many other structures that require the attention of a skilled preservationist, before they fall into total disrepair and eventual destruction.

Criss-Cross Rhode Island!

There are many exciting forts and historic battle sites in Rhode Island. The Fort Ningret State Historic Site in Charlestown contains the original outline of a fort that the Dutch built before the first Pilgrim settlers landed at Plymouth in 1620! Queen's Fort State Historic Site near Exeter contains the ruins of an ancient Native American fort that was abandoned in 1676. Fort Adams State Park in Newport preserves massive granite walls, tunnels, and powder magazines that were built to protect Narragansett Bay. Fort Adams is also one of the largest seacoast fortifications in the United States! Fort Getty on Conanicut Island contains amazing Revolutionary War earthen barriers. Gaspee Point is the site of the daring capture of the British ship *Gaspee*, just before the colonists declared war on the British!

Use the information above to complete the crossword below!

ACROSS

1. You'll see earthen barriers from the Revolutionary War at Fort _____ State Park.

2. Fort _____ in Newport was built to protect Narragansett Bay.

3. You can trace the outline of a very old Dutch fort at Fort _____ State Historic site.

DOWN

1. _____ Point is the site where colonists captured and burned a British schooner just before the American Revolution was declared.

4. Queens _____ in Exeter is the site of a Native American fort.

ANSWERS: ACROSS: 1. Getty; 2-Adams; 3-Ningret; DOWN: 1-Gaspee; 4-Fort

©2001 Carole Marsh/Gallopade International/800-536-2GET/www.rhodeislandexperience.com/Page 23

Rhode Island Rules!

In 1841, ratification of the People's Constitution reforms voting requirements.

In 1935, major governmental reorganization, known as the "Bloodless Revolution," cements Democratic rule for more than 20 years.

In 1977, the state establishes department of environmental management.

Use the code to complete the sentences.

A	B	C	D	E	F	G	H	I	J	K	L	M	N	O	P
1	2	3	4	5	6	7	8	9	10	11	12	13	14	15	16

Q	R	S	T	U	V	W	X	Y	Z
17	18	19	20	21	22	23	24	25	26

1. State rules are called __ __ __ __ .
   12 1 23 19

2. Laws are made in our state __ __ __ __ __ __ __ .
   3 1 16 9 20 15 12

3. The leader of our state is the __ __ __ __ __ __ __ __ .
   7 15 22 5 18 14 15 18

4. We live in the state of __ __ __ __ __   __ __ __ __ __ __ .
   18 8 15 4 5   9 19 12 1 14 4

5. The capital of our state is __ __ __ __ __ __ __ __ __ __ .
   16 18 15 22 9 4 5 14 3 5

R H O D E I S L A N D ! ! !

ANSWERS: 1-laws; 2-capitol; 3-governor; 4-Rhode Island; 5-Providence

©2001 Carole Marsh/Gallopade International/800-536-2GET/www.rhodeislandexperience.com/Page 24

Buzzing Around Rhode Island!

Write the answers to the questions below. To get to the beehive, follow a path through the maze.

1. The capital of Rhode Island is _____.
2. Oceanfront mansions are located in _____.
3. _____ is the city which means "place by a waterfall."
4. _____ Island is also known as Jamestown.
5. _____ is considered Rhode Island's second settlement after Providence.
6. Some of Rhode Island's best beaches can be found in _____, the state's largest town.
7. This town is located in the "westerly" part of the state. _____
8. _____ was once known as the Town of 10 Churches.
9. _____ is a picture-perfect New England town complete with a village green, surrounded by a church and municipal buildings.
10. _____ Island was first discovered by Giovanni da Verrazzano, one of the first European explorers to reach present-day Rhode Island.

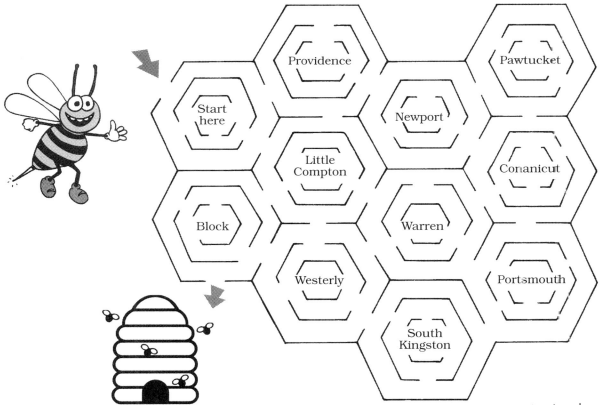

ANSWERS: 1-Providence; 2-Newport; 3-Pawtucket; 4-Conanicut; 5-Portsmouth; 6-South Kingston; 7-Westerly; 8-Warren; 9-Little Compton; 10-Block

©2001 Carole Marsh/Gallopade International/800-536-2GET/www.rhodeislandexperience.com/Page 25

Rhode Island Through the Years!

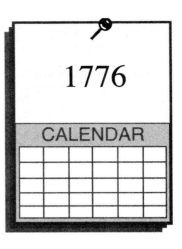

Many great things have happened in Rhode Island throughout its history. Chronicle the following important Rhode Island events by solving math problems to find out the years in which they happened.

1. Giovanni da Verrazzano sails into present-day Narragansett Bay

    5 X 3= ____   8 X 3= ____

2. Roger Williams arrives in what is now Rhode Island and founds Providence

    4 X 4= ____   9 X 4= ____

3. Williams receives charter for Rhode Island

    8 X 2= ____   11 X 4= ____

4. Native Americans attack Rhode Island settlers but are eventually defeated

    8 X 2= ____   25 X 3= ____

5. Rhode Island becomes first colony to renounce allegiance to England

    20-3= ____   4 X 18= ____

6. Rhode Islanders are forbidden by law to trade slaves

    15+2= ____   90-3= ____

7. U.S. Navy opens Newport Naval Station

    9 X 2= ____   86-3= ____

8. Hurricane strikes Rhode Island, killing about 250 people and causing millions of dollars in property damage

    25-6= ____   42-4= ____

ANSWERS: 1-1524; 2-1636; 3-1644; 4-1675; 5-1772; 6-1787; 7-1883; 8-1938

©2001 Carole Marsh/Gallopade International/800-536-2GET/www.rhodeislandexperience.com/Page 26

What Did We Do Before Money?

In early Rhode Island, there were no banks. However, people still wanted to barter, trade, or otherwise "purchase" goods from each other. Wampum, made of shells, bone, or stones, was often swapped for goods. Indians, especially, used wampum for "money." In the barter system, people swapped goods or services.

Later, banks came into existence, and people began to use money to buy goods. However, they also still bartered when they had no money to spend.

Place a star in the box below the systems used today.

©2001 Carole Marsh/Gallopade International/800-536-2GET/www.rhodeislandexperience.com/Page 27

Rhymin' Riddles

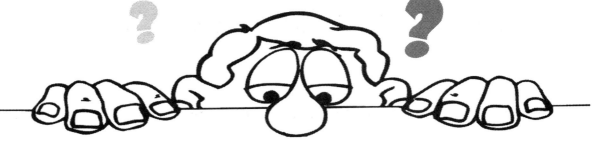

for Famous Folk

1. My job as an artist brought me great fame;
   A portrait of George Washington is signed with my name.

   Who am I? _____ _____

2. From Boston I fled astride a white bull;
   I'm the "Sage of the Wilderness," with knowledge, I'm full!

   Who am I? _____ _____

3. I'm Providence-born and Yankee bred;
   I served in the Senate, and Governor's stead.

   Who am I? _____ _____ _____

4. I have fun with the puck, I can skate like the wind;
   My game is hockey, to the Olympics I've been.

   Who am I? _____ _____

ANSWERS: 1-Gilbert Stuart; 2-William Blackstone; 3-Theodore Francis Green; 4-Mathieu Schneider

Rhode Island Map Symbols!

Make up symbols for these names and draw them in the space provided on the right.

Factory	
Christmas trees	
Fish	
Sailboats	
Mansion	
Navy ship	
Bridge	
Quahogs or clams	

©2001 Carole Marsh/Gallopade International/800-536-2GET/www.rhodeislandexperience.com/Page 29

Rhode Island Goodies!

Most of Rhode Island's income from agriculture comes from growing shrubs for landscaping Christmas trees, and turf (seeded soil).

The second most important agricultural products include milk and dairy foods.

Other farm products include chickens, potatoes, and turkeys.

Match the name of each crop or product from Rhode Island with the picture of that item.

Sweet Corn   Potatoes   Milk
Apples   Snap Beans   Grapes

©2001 Carole Marsh/Gallopade International/800-536-2GET/www.rhodeislandexperience.com/Page 30

Historical Rhode Island Women World Wonders!

Rhode Island has been the home of many brave and influential women. See if you can match these women with their accomplishments.

- A. Jemima Wilkinson
- B. Elizabeth Buffum Chace
- C. Sarah Doyle
- D. Katharine Gibbs
- E. Christiana Cartreax Bannister

1. ___ She helped organize women's clubs and opened the door for women's admissions at Brown University.

2. ___ She started a chain of secretarial schools.

3. ___ She was a teacher and religious leader.

4. ___ She owned hairdressing businesses and worked for social causes.

5. ___ She was a Quaker matron and political activist in the early 1800s.

6. ___ Her first school was opened in Providence in 1911.

7. ___ A fever in 1776 caused her to have a "vision" that convinced her to preach.

8. ___ Much of her life was spent helping the less fortunate.

9. ___ She helped to establish the Rhode Island School of Design.

10. ___ She worked for better conditions for women prisoners and helped establish a school for homeless children.

ANSWERS: 1-C; 2-D; 3-A; 4-E; 5-B; 6-D; 7-A; 8-E; 9-C; 10-B

Producers and Consumers

Producers (sellers) make goods or provide services. Ralph, a fourth grade student in Corning, is a consumer because he wants to buy a new wheel for his bicycle. Other products and services from Rhode Island that consumers can buy include jewelry and silverware production, fabricated metal products, textiles, and scientific instruments.

- Manufacturing has been important to Rhode Island's economy since the early 1800s.

- Production of jewelry and silverware has been important since the 1700s

- Small manufactured goods like valves, screws, metal pipe fittings, nails and hand tools are second in importance.

- Providence, Rhode Island's capital, is an important wholesale trade center.

- Rhode Island's port facilities enhance its position as an international trade center.

Complete these sentences.

Without hammers and nails, I couldn't

_____

_____

Without scientific calculators, I couldn't

_____

_____

Without textiles or fabrics, I couldn't

_____

_____

Without silverware, I couldn't

_____

_____

Rhode Island Word Wheel!

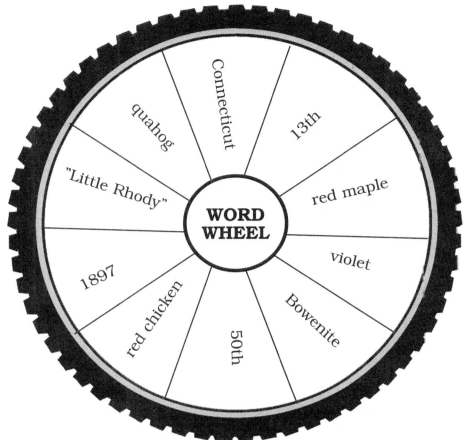

Use the Word Wheel of Rhode Island names to complete the sentences below.

1. The state bird is the Rhode Island _____.
2. The state tree is the _____.
3. The state shell is the _____.
4. The state flower is the _____.
5. Rhode Island became the _____ state to join the union on May 29, 1790.
6. One of the state's nicknames is _____.
7. Rhode Island adopted its state flag in _____.
8. The state mineral is _____.
9. _____ lies along Rhode Island's western border.
10. Rhode Island ranks _____ in size among the states.

ANSWERS: 1-red chicken; 2-red maple; 3-quahog; 4-violet; 5-13th; 6-"Little Rhody"; 7-1897; 8-Bowenite; 9-Connecticut; 13-50th

©2001 Carole Marsh/Gallopade International/800-536-2GET/www.rhodeislandexperience.com/Page 33

Running Across Rhode Island!

It's easy to run across Rhode Island from east to west when it's only 37 miles (60 kilometers) wide! **Trace your trip on the map below.**

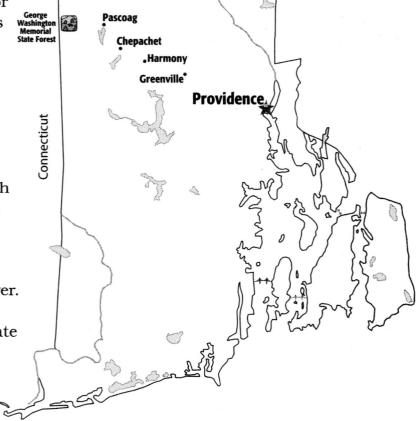

- Start out on the Connecticut border and begin jogging east along Rhode Island State Highway #44. Your first stop will be in the George Washington Memorial State Forest, west of Pascoag. Look for some red maples, Rhode Island's state tree, while you're there!
- Tie up your running shoes and head east for Chepachet. Stop in at The Brown & Hopkins Country Store for some old-time penny candy!
- Continue following Highway #44 slightly southeast until you reach the town of Harmony. Kick back and take a water break.
- Jogging southeast, stop in Greenville and pick some pretty violets, Rhode Island's state flower.
- The last stretch of your run will take you into Providence, the state capital. Find a park bench and relax on Riverwalk, beside the Woonasquatucket River.

©2001 Carole Marsh/Gallopade International/800-536-2GET/www.rhodeislandexperience.com/Page 34

Create Your Own Rhode Island State Quarter!

Look at the change in your pocket. You might notice that one of the coins has changed. The United States is minting new quarters, one for each of the 50 states. Each quarter has a design on it that says something special about one particular state. The Rhode Island quarter was released in January 2001, and is in cash registers and piggy banks everywhere!

What if you had designed the Rhode Island quarter? Draw a picture of how you would like the Rhode Island quarter to look. Make sure you include things that are special about Rhode Island.

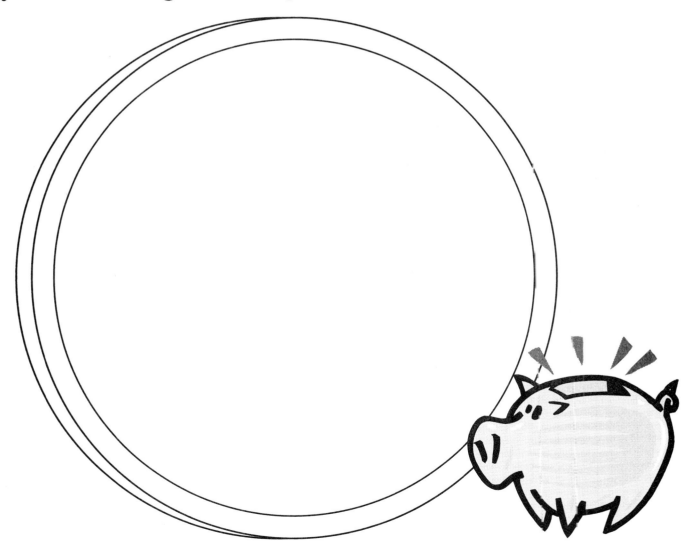

©2001 Carole Marsh/Gallopade International/800-536-2GET/www.rhodeislandexperience.com/Page 35

Rhode Island Law Comes In Many Flavors!

For each of these people, write down the kind(s) of law used to decide whether their actions are legal or illegal.

1. Bank robber _____

2. Business person _____

3. State park ranger _____

4. Rhode Islanders _____

5. Doctor _____

6. Real estate agent _____

7. Corporate president _____

8. Ship owner _____

9. Diplomat _____

10. Soldier _____

Medical Law

International Law

Military Law

Commercial Law

Maritime Law

Antitrust Law

Criminal Law

State Law

Environmental Law

Property Law

ANSWERS: (May vary slightly) 1-Criminal; 2-Commercial; 3-Environmental; 4-State; 5-Medical; 6-Property; 7-Antitrust; 8-Maritime; 9-International; 10-Military

©2001 Carole Marsh/Gallopade International/800-536-2GET/www.rhodeislandexperience.com/Page 36

Mixed-Up States!

Color, cut out, and paste each of Rhode Island's two neighbors onto the map below.

Be sure and match the state shapes!

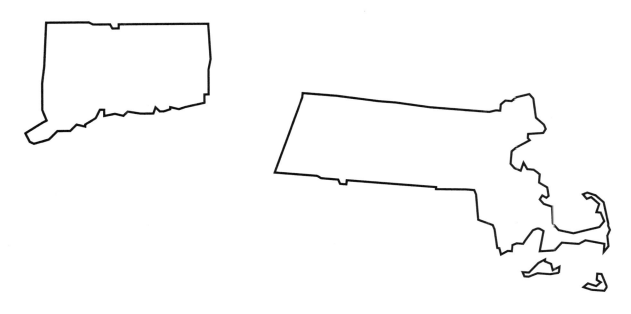

©2001 Carole Marsh/Gallopade International/800-536-2GET/www.rhodeislandexperience.com/Page 37

Sailing Away, Rhode Island Style!

Yacht racing is one of the unofficial sports that come to mind when you think of Rhode Island. Newport was the site of America's Cup races for more than 30 years, and still hosts the Newport to Bermuda Races, and several other prestigious events. Weekend sailing enthusiasts regularly hoist their sails for club-sponsored regattas.

When you're on board any kind of boat, you have to use special terms to talk about directions. Label the ship below with these terms:

bow: front of the ship
stern: back of the ship
fore: towards the bow
aft: towards the stern
port: left as you face the bow
starboard: right as you face the bow

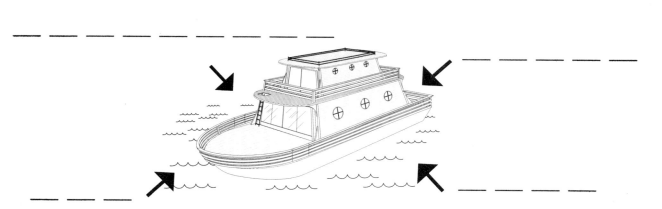

This arrow is pointing _ _ _ _ _ .

This arrow is pointing _ _ _ _

This arrow is pointing _ _ _ _ .

Rhode Island Politics As Usual!

Our elected government officials decide how much money is going to be spent on schools, roads, public parks, and libraries. It's very important for the citizens of Rhode Island to understand what's going on in their government, and how it will affect them. Rhode Island's present constitution is its second governing document in its history; however, many important amendments were added in 1988 following a constitutional convention.

Before the 19th Amendment to the U.S. Constitution, women were unable to vote in the United States. In 1920, enough states ratified the 19th Amendment, and it became the law of the land. Women gained total suffrage nationally, and continue to be a major force in the election process today. Elizabeth Buffum Chace was one of Rhode Island's activists, fighting for women's rights and against slavery. Isabelle Ahearn O'Neill became Rhode Island's first woman legislator after being elected to the House of Representatives two years (1922) after women got the right to vote.

On the lines provided, write down a question for each of the answers below. A hint follows each answer.

1. Question: _____
   Answer: A draft of a law presented for review.
   (Short for William!)

2. Question: _____
   Answer: The right to vote.
   (Don't make us suffer!)

3. Question: _____
   Answer: The ability to forbid a bill or law from being passed.
   (Just say no!)

4. Question: _____
   Answer: The fundamental law of the United States that was framed in 1787 and put into effect in 1789.
   (Rhode Island has one too!)

5. Question: _____
   Answer: An amendment.
   (It's not something subtracted from #4!)

ANSWERS: (may vary slightly) 1-What is a bill? 2-What is suffrage? 3-What is a veto? 4-What is the Constitution? 5-What is an addition to the Constitution called?

What Shall I Be When I Grow Up?

Here are just a few of the jobs that kept early Rhode Islanders busy.

Lawyer	Carpenter	Baker
Tenant Farmer	Weaver	Pharmacist
Woodcarver	Barber	Gaoler (jailer)
Judge	Gardener	Fisherman
Housekeeper	Mantuamaker (dressmaker)	Doctor
Silversmith	Printer	Governor
Politician	Cook	Milliner (hatmaker)
Dairyman	Musician	Soldier
Wheelwright	Bookbinder	Hunter
Teacher	Laundress	Blacksmith
Servant	Jeweler	Sailor
Cabinetmaker	Innkeeper	Beekeeper
Mayor	Stablehand	Gunsmith
Plantation Owner	Tailor	Prospector

You are a young colonist trying to decide what you want to be when you grow up.

Choose a career and next to it write a description of what you think you would do each day as a:

Write your career choice here!

Write your career choice here!

Write your career choice here!

Write your career choice here!

©2001 Carole Marsh/Gallopade International/800-536-2GET/www.rhodeislandexperience.com/Page 40

Rhode Island's Governor!

The governor is the leader of the state.

You've been assigned to write a biography of the governor of Rhode Island.

Before you can start your book, you need to jot down some notes in your trusty computer. Fill in the necessary information in the spaces provided on the dossier!

GOVERNOR'S NAME:

_____

_____

Date of Birth:

Place of Birth:

Father:

Mother:

Siblings:

Spouse:

Children:

Pets:

Schools Attended:

Previous Occupation(s):

Likes:

Dislikes:

abc • APPLICATIONS   MENU   CALCULATOR   FIND   123

©2001 Carole Marsh/Gallopade International/800-536-2GET/www.rhodeislandexperience.com/Page 41

The ORIGINAL Native Rhode Islanders!

Archaeologists believe that the first people came to Rhode Island about 12,000 years ago. They lived mainly by hunting deer, growing corn, and catching fish and shellfish. These ancient people migrated between the inland and coastal areas. Their villages were led by a chief called a *sachem*, and villages sometimes joined together to form confederacies. Later, several groups of Algonquian-speaking Native Americans inhabited what is now the state of Rhode Island.

What kinds of things did Native Americans use in their everyday life? For each of the things shown, circle YES if Native Americans did use it, or NO if they didn't.

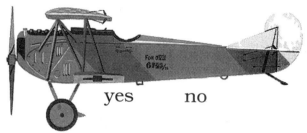
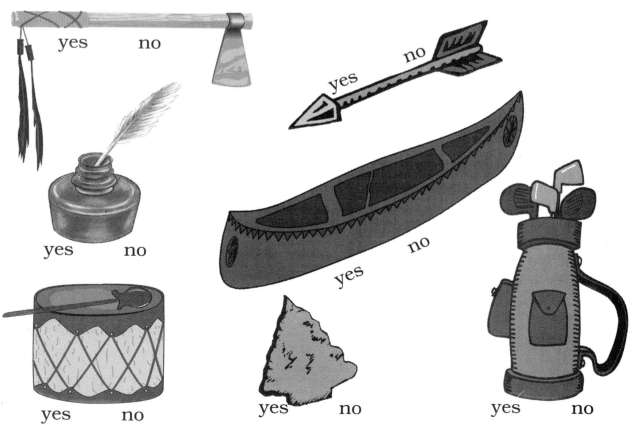

All Around Rhode Island Code-Buster!

Decipher the code and write in the names of the states and bodies of water that border Rhode Island.

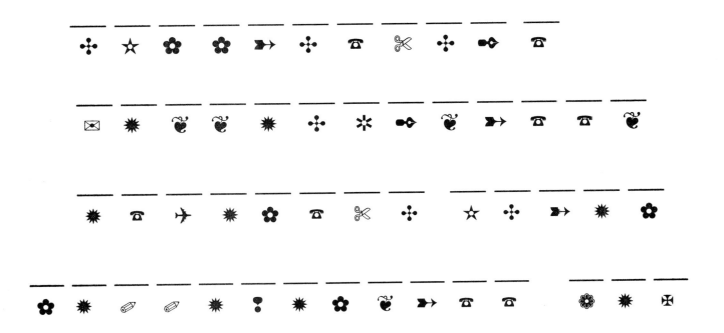

ANSWERS: 1-Connecticut; 2-Massachusetts; Atlantic Ocean; Narragansett Bay

Unique Rhode Island Place Names!

Can you figure out the compound words that make up the names of these Rhode Island places?

Newport   _____   _____

Nooseneck   _____   _____

Charlestown   _____   _____

Wickford   _____   _____

Lakewood   _____   _____

Oakland   _____   _____

Portsmouth   _____   _____

Riverside   _____   _____

Smithfield   _____   _____

Wakefield   _____   _____

ANSWERS: New/port; Noose/neck; Charles/town; Wick/ford; Lake/wood; Oak/land; Ports/mouth; River/side; Smith/field; Wake/field

©2001 Carole Marsh/Gallopade International/800-536-2GET/www.rhodeislandexperience.com/Page 44

Looking For a Home in the Ocean State!

Can you figure out where these things, people, and animals belong?

1. governor
2. professor
3. sand castle builder
4. lighthouse keeper
5. park ranger
6. factory worker
7. sailor
8. professional tennis player
9. stevedore
10. silversmith

A. Providence
B. Block Island
C. Pawtucket
D. Newport Casino
E. Port of Providence
F. Brown University
G. Naval War College
H. State Capitol
I. Beavertail State Park
J. Narragansett Beach

ANSWERS: 1-H; 2-F; 3-J; 4-B; 5-I; 6-C; 7-G; 8-D; 9-E; 10-A

©2001 Carole Marsh/Gallopade International/800-536-2GET/www.rhodeislandexperience.com/Page 45

I Love Rhode Island, Weather or Not!

Rhode Island has a humid continental climate that is fairly wet. An annual amount of precipitation (rain and snow) is about 44 inches (112 centimeters). Breezes from the Atlantic Ocean and Narragansett Bay keep Rhode Island's climate fairly moderate, preventing extreme hot or cold temperatures. Its temperatures usually average 29°F (-2°C) in the winter and about 71°F (22°C) in the summer.

The highest temperature on record is 104°F (40°C) in Providence on August 2, 1975. The lowest temperature recorded to date is -23°F (-31°C), Kingston, January 11, 1942.

On the thermometer gauges below, color the mercury red (°F) to show the hottest temperature ever recorded in Rhode Island. Color the mercury blue (°F) to show the coldest temperature ever recorded in Rhode Island.

In 1978, a great blizzard immobilized the state.

Temperatures are several degrees warmer in summer and several degrees colder in winter along Rhode Island's south shore.

An unusual pattern for snowstorms can deposit three times as much snow in northern Rhode Island as in other parts of the state.

Hurricanes strike the state on an average of one every 10-15 years.

©2001 Carole Marsh/Gallopade International/800-536-2GET/www.rhodeislandexperience.com/Page 46

The Scenic Route

Imagine that you've planned an exciting exploratory expedition around Rhode Island for your classmates. You've chosen some cities and other places to take your friends.

Circle these sites and cities on the map below, then number them in the order you would visit if you were traveling north to south through the state:

____ Peace Dale

____ Watch Hill

____ Lighthouse at Warwick

____ Odeum movie theater in East Greenwich

____ Providence Children's Museum

____ Wickford

____ Narragansett Indian reservation, Charlestown

____ Dame farm in Cranston

ANSWERS: 1-Providence; 2-Cranston; 3-Warwick; 4-East Greenwich; 5-Wickford; 6-Peace Dale; 7-Charlestown; 8-Watch Hill

©2001 Carole Marsh/Gallopade International/800-536-2GET/www.rhodeislandexperience.com/Page 47

Key to a Map!

A map key, also called a map legend, shows symbols which represent different things on a map.

Match each word with a symbol for things found in the state of Rhode Island.

Airport - Theodore Francis Green Airport

Church - Grace Church, Providence

River - Seekonk

Road - Ocean Drive, Newport

School - Brown University

State capital - Providence

Battle site - Gaspee Point

Aviary - Roger Williams Park

©2001 Carole Marsh/Gallopade International/800-536-2GET/www.rhodeislandexperience.com/Page 48

BROTHER, CAN YOU SPARE A DIME?

After the collapse of the stock market on Wall Street in 1929, the state of Rhode Island, along with the rest of the nation, plunged headfirst into the Great Depression. It was the worst economic crisis America had ever known. Banks closed and businesses crashed...there was financial ruin everywhere.

Even before the depression, Rhode Island's textile industry was slowing down and mills were closed. Many plants moved south where labor was cheaper and overhead costs were lower. Other manufacturing plants closed during the Great Depression or workers were forced to accept lower wages.

Our President Helps

While the nation was in the midst of the Depression, Franklin Delano Roosevelt became president. With America on the brink of economic devastation, the federal government stepped forward and hired unemployed people to build parks, bridges, and roads. With this help, and other government assistance, the country began to slowly, and painfully, pull out of the Great Depression. Within the first 100 days of his office, Roosevelt enacted a number of policies to help minimize the suffering of the nation's many unemployed workers. These programs were known as the NEW DEAL. The jobs helped families support themselves and improved the country's infrastructure.

Put an X next to the jobs that were part of Roosevelt's New Deal.

1. computer programmer _____
2. bridge builder _____
3. fashion model _____
4. park builder _____
5. interior designer _____
6. hospital builder _____
7. school builder _____
8. website designer _____

ANSWERS: 2, 4, 6, 7

Rhode Island Newcomers!

People have come to Rhode Island from other states and many other countries on almost every continent! As time goes by, Rhode Island's population grows more diverse. This means that people of different races and from different cultures and ethnic backgrounds have moved to Rhode Island.

In the past, many immigrants have come to Rhode Island from Ireland. More recently, people have migrated to Rhode Island from Eastern Europe and southeast Asia. Only a certain number of immigrants are allowed to move to America each year. Many of these immigrants eventually become U.S. citizens.

Read the statement and decide if it's a fact or an opinion. Write your answer on the line.

_____ 1. Many of Rhode Island's early immigrants came from Europe.

_____ 2. Lots of immigrants speak a language other than English.

_____ 3. The clothing immigrants wear is very interesting.

_____ 4. Immigrants from England have a neat accent when they speak.

_____ 5. Many immigrants will become United States citizens.

_____ 6. People have immigrated to Rhode Island from nearly every country in the world.

An immigrant is a person who migrates to another country in hopes of a better life.

ANSWERS: 1-fact; 2-fact; 3-opinion; 4-opinion; 5-fact; 6-fact

A Day in the Life of a Settler!

Pretend you are a settler in the days of early Rhode Island. You keep a diary of what you do each day. Write in the "diary" what you might have done on a long, hot summer day in July 1643.

Home, Sweet Home!

Rhode Island has been home to many different authors, poets, and other writers. Here are just a few. See if you can locate their hometowns on the map of Rhode Island below!

Write the number of each writer by his or her hometown on the map.

1. Leonard Bacon—poet, awarded the Pulitzer Prize for *Sunderland Capture and Other Poems* in 1941. *Hint: lived in a town that starts with "P" and rhymes with "geese pail"*

2. Julia Ward Howe—wrote text for "The Battle Hymn of the Republic;" writer, reformer, and poet. *Hint: lived on island; compound word meaning "not old" harbor*

3. Howard Phillips "H.P." Lovecraft—short story writer and novelist; wrote *The Whisperer in Darkness* and *The Thing on the Doorstep* *Hint: Lived in the capital city*

4. Janet Taylor Lisle—children's author; wrote *The Art of Keeping Cool* and *The Great Dimpole Oak*. *Hint: Her hometown rhymes with "river fun"*

5. Avi—wrote *Man Who Was Poe* and *Something Upstairs: A Tale of Ghosts*. *Hint: His hometown is the city that means divine guidance or care*

6. David Macauley—wrote *The Way Things Work, Castle, Black and White,* and *Cathedral*. *Hint: his hometown is another word for a place where rabbits breed*

7. Chris Van Allsburg—wrote *Jumanji* and *Polar Express*, both Caldecott Winners. *Hint: hometown is the same as Lovecraft's and Avi's*

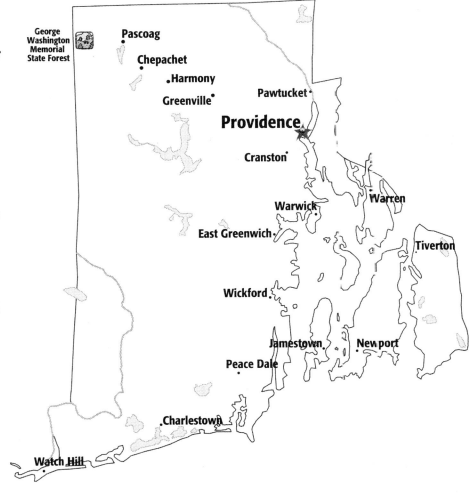

ANSWERS: 1-Peace Dale; 2-Newport; 3-Providence; 4-Tiverton; 5-Providence; 6-Warren; 7-Providence

Rhode Island Spelling Bee!

Good spelling is a good habit. Study the words on the left side of the page. Then fold the page in half and "take a spelling test" on the right side. Have a buddy read the words aloud to you. When finished, unfold the page and check your spelling. Keep your score. GOOD LUCK.

Each word is worth 5 points.

- arcade _____
- carousel _____
- climate _____
- coastal _____
- ferryboats _____
- hockey _____
- lighthouses _____
- mansion _____
- manufacturing _____
- mill _____
- molasses _____
- museum _____
- Newport _____
- Portsmouth _____
- Providence _____
- quahog _____
- salt ponds _____
- tavern _____
- textiles _____
- yacht _____

A perfect score is 100! How many did you get right?

©2001 Carole Marsh/Gallopade International/800-536-2GET/www.rhodeislandexperience.com/Page 54

Naturally Rhode Island!

Fill in the bubblegram with some Rhode Island crops and natural resources. Use the letter clues to help you.

- Water is probably Rhode Island's greatest natural resource.
- There is an abundance of fish and shellfish in the state's waters.
- Glacial movements during the great Ice Age, provided Rhode Island with minerals such as coal, graphite, quartzite, and bog iron.
- Westerly granite is prized as an excellent building stone.

WORD BANK
lobster   clams
granite   limestone
sandstone   quartzite
sand   gravel

1. O _ _ _ S
2. G _ _ O _ _ _
3. Q _ _ O _ _ _ _ _ O
4. O _ O D
5. L O _ _ _ _ _
6. S O _ _ _ OO _ _
7. _ _ _ O _ L
8. _ O _ _ _ _ _ O E

Now unscramble the "bubble" letters to find out the mystery word!
HINT: What is one way we can help to save our environment?

_ _ _ _ _ _ _ _ _ _ _ _

ANSWERS: 1- clams; 2-granite; 3-quartzite; 4-sand; 5-lobster; 6-sandstone; 7-gravel; 8-limestone
MYSTERY WORD: conservation

Alphabetically Speaking in Rhode Island!

Rhode Island is probably best known for industry. Shipbuilding and commerce were the major economic activities in Rhode Island in the late 17th century. Eventually, Rhode Island became the first state to industrialize and was the site of the first successful cotton mill. It was the first state to use waterpower to drive machinery. This revolutionized American manufacturing and the way Americans worked. The growing need for labor in the textile mills also brought a new wave of immigrants to Rhode Island in search of jobs.

Alphabetize the following words by numbering them from 1 to 10.

____industry

____shipbuilding

____labor

____century

____cotton

____textiles

____mill

____immigrant

____successful

____wave

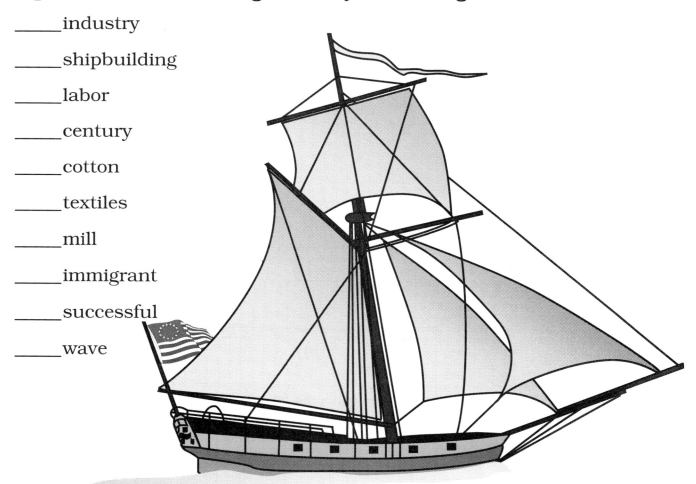

ANSWERS: 1-century; 2-cotton; 3-immigrants; 4-industry; 5-labor; 6-mill; 7-shipbuilding; 8-successful; 9-textiles; 10-wave

©2001 Carole Marsh/Gallopade International/800-536-2GET/www.rhodeislandexperience.com/Page 56

What a Great Idea!

The water-run machines operated 24-hours a day

David Wilkinson manufactured tools and equipment in a mill that opened in 1810.

Rhode Island's industrial revolution began in Pawtucket

Slater sneaked out of England with the plan for the Arkwright textile machine committed to memory

WORD BANK
Aaron Lopez
George Henry Corliss
Moses Brown
Samuel Slater
Zachariah Allen

1. _____ built the first water-powered textile mill to manufacture cotton thread.

2. _____ is considered the "Father of the American textile industry" and built the first waterpowered spinning machine.

3. _____ was a candlemaker who produced spermaceti candles from whale by-products.

4. _____ was an American inventor who is known for developing the steam engine.

5. _____ engineered reservoirs to provide running water for mill operation during drought seasons.

ANSWERS: 1-Moses Brown; 2-Samuel Slater; 3-Aaron Lopez; 4-George Henry Corliss; 5-Zachariah Allen

Famous Rhode Islander Scavenger Hunt!

Here is a list of some of the famous people associated with our state. **Go on a scavenger hunt to see if you can "capture" a fact about each one. Use an encyclopedia, almanac, or other resource you might need. Happy hunting!**

Nelson Wilmarth Aldrich _____

Edward Bannister _____

John Brown _____

John Carter Brown _____

Moses Brown _____

Nicholas Brown _____

Ambrose Burnside _____

Ruth Ann Buzzi _____

George Michael Cohan _____

Thomas Wilson Dorr _____

Eddie Dowling _____

Theodore Francis Green _____

Stephen Hopkins _____

Julia Ward Howe _____

Edward Benjamin Koren _____

Napoleon "Nap" Lajoie _____

Irving R. Levine _____

Howard Phillips "H.P." Lovecraft _____

Horace Mann Gilbert Stuart _____

Roger Williams _____

Finding Pirate Kidd's Coins

Use the words in the circles to fill in the blanks in this Rhode Island story. Some may be used more than once.

WORD BANK
thieving
Jamestown
hanged
coin
loot

Could Pirate Captain William Kidd's _____ still be buried on Conanicut Island, present-day Jamestown? It's anybody's guess, but local lore holds that Kidd's _____ comrade, Thomas Paine, may have held the _____ for him while he sailed up the coast to Boston. Unfortunately for Kidd, he was arrested and _____ upon his arrival and never returned to _____. A golden _____ was found in Paine's house when it was renovated, but the bulk of the booty was never recovered!

©2001 Carole Marsh/Gallopade International/800-536-2GET/www.rhodeislandexperience.com/Page 59

Map of North America

This is a map of North America. Rhode Island is one of the 50 states.

Color the state of Rhode Island red.

Color the rest of the United States yellow. Alaska and Hawaii are part of the United States and should also be colored yellow.

Color Canada green. Color Mexico blue.

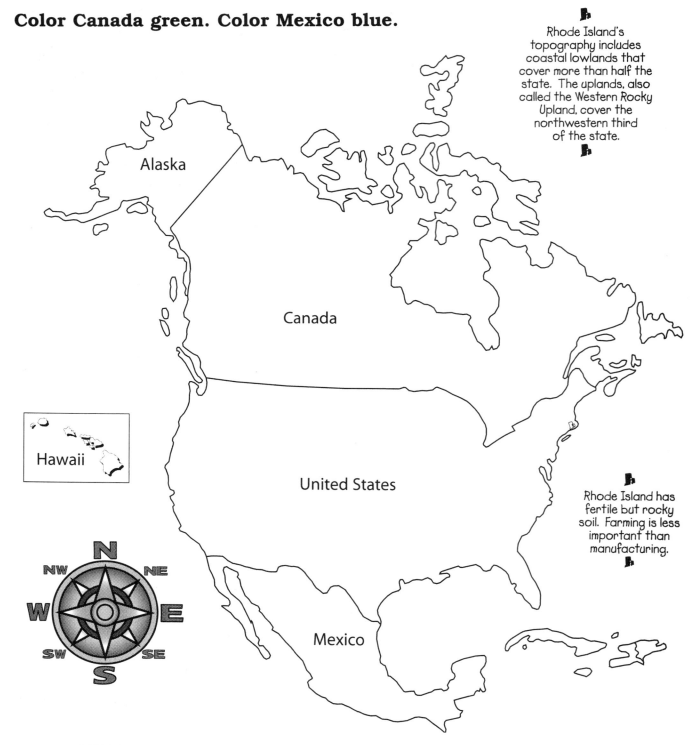

Rhode Island's topography includes coastal lowlands that cover more than half the state. The uplands, also called the Western Rocky Upland, cover the northwestern third of the state.

Rhode Island has fertile but rocky soil. Farming is less important than manufacturing.

©2001 Carole Marsh/Gallopade International/800-536-2GET/www.rhodeislandexperience.com/Page 60

Newport— Home of the Rich and Famous!

True or False?!

Newport is often called America's First Resort. The sea and natural beauty of Newport is what drew its first visitors in the 18th century. Later the rich and powerful members of New York society who built about 60 "summer cottages" discovered it. These "cottages" were actually multi-million-dollar mansions, along its coast. Some of the most famous mansions include The Breakers, the summer home of Cornelius Vanderbilt; Rosecliff; The Elms; Marble House; and Belcourt Castle. Not only was Newport the "first resort," it was also the home of the first U.S. post office, the first free public school, the first U.S. synagogue, and the first open gold tournament!

Read each sentence, and decide if it is TRUE or FALSE. Write your answers on the lines provided.

1. Newport's shopping centers are what first drew visitors in the 18th century.

_____

2. Newport's "summer cottages" are actually multi-million dollar mansions built by wealthy industrialists.

_____

3. The sea is one of Newport's natural resources.

_____

4. Newport's first tourists arrived in the 19th century.

_____

5. The names of some of Newport's famous mansions include The Breakers, Rosecliff, and Marble House.

_____

ANSWERS: 1-false; 2-true; 3-true; 4-false; 5-true

©2001 Carole Marsh/Gallopade International/800-536-2GET/www.rhodeislandexperience.com/Page 61

Rhode Island State Greats!

In the paragraph about important people from Rhode Island below there are eight misspelled words. Circle the misspelled words, and then spell them correctly on the lines provided.

The Brown family of Rhode Island made important contibutions to the educational, economic, and artistic growth of their state and the nation. John Brown was a shipping merchent who made his forchune in the 1700s through slave trading and privateering. He outfited and supplied the Continental Army in the American Revolution. Nicholas Brown was a merchant who fonded Rhode Island College. This institution was renamed Brown Univarsity in his honor. Another Brown, John Carter, donated a collecshun of American buks to Brown University where the libary was named for him.

ANSWERS: merchant; fortune; outfitted; founded; University; collection; books; library

Virtual Rhode Island!

It's time to build your own website! We've given you pictures of things that have to do with Rhode Island. Color and cut them out, and arrange them on a blank piece of paper to create a web page that will make people want to visit Rhode Island!

©2001 Carole Marsh/Gallopade International/800-536-2GET/www.rhodeislandexperience.com/Page 63

Tiverton's Talking Rocks!

Can rocks really talk? Maybe not in words but certainly in pictures! Tiverton's "Speaking rocks" have been a curiosity to Rhode Islanders since they were discovered on Fogland Beach. There were originally a half dozen carved boulders, but only one remains. The rest were claimed either by the sea or by scavengers.

The hieroglyphics featured on the rocks are attributed to the Norsemen, Native Americans, or other early explorers, but no positive identification has ever been made.

Read each sentence, and decide if it is FACT or FICTION. Write your answers on the lines provided.

1. Rocks can "talk" in pictures.

2. Tiverton's speaking rocks are real boulders with carved pictures that tell a story.

3. Hieroglyphics are pictures that tell a story.

4. Boulders are large rocks.

5. The "speaking rocks" can laugh out loud!

ANSWERS: 1-fact; 2-fact; 3-fact; 4-fact; 5-fiction

©2001 Carole Marsh/Gallopade International/800-536-2GET/www.rhodeislandexperience.com/Page 64

A River Runs Through It!

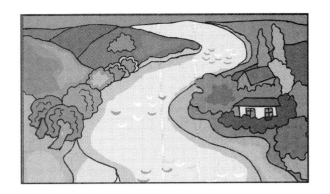

RIVER BANK

Blackstone

Seekonk

Woonsaquatucket

Providence

Pawcatuck

The state of Rhode Island is blessed with many rivers. See if you can wade right in and figure out these rivers' names!

For each river code, circle every other letter (beginning with the second one) to discover the name!

1. The color of this river is dark as night and heavy as a rock.

   X B Z L G A M C F K I S P T H O V N J E

2. The first part of this river's name is one of the seven senses. The next syllable sounds like a marine creature that lives in a shell.

   V S A E F E X K I O G N H K

3. A feline has four of these. Feline is another name for cat. Now that you know the first two syllables of this river's name, just "tuck" this page away.

   O P J A E W I C X A L T D U Z C M K

4. The name of this river means wisdom, care, and guidance provided by God.

   B P F R H O J V K I L D A E M N Z C X E

5. A five-syllable name that rhymes with "loon-in-a-bucket"

   B W M O A O K N L S H A X Q D U Q A N T C U J C O K D E X T

ANSWERS: 1-Blackstone; 2-Seekonk; 3-Pawcatuck; 4-Providence; 5-Woonsaquatucket

Rhode Island Firsts!

Rhode Island has had a lot of firsts. Here are just a few!

Not So New Newport!

Newport is sometimes called America's First Resort.

First Spud!

The first "Mr. Potato Head™" was made in Pawtucket by Hasbro toy company in 1952.

Milling Around!

Rhode Island is the home of the first water-operated textile mill in the United States, started in 1793.

Small but Proud!

Rhode Island is the smallest state in the Union. It was the first of the original 13 colonies to declare its independence from Great Britain in 1776, but the last to ratify the U.S. Constitution in 1790.

Which "first" happened first? Circle the first "first"!

 First to Declare Independence

 First Mr. Potato Head™

 First Water-Operated Textile Mill

ANSWERS: 1776 Rhode Island declares independence from Great Britain

Rhode Island Gazetteer

A gazetteer is a list of places. For each of these famous Rhode Island places, write down the town in which it's located, and one interesting fact about the place. You may have to use an encyclopedia, almanac, or other resource to find the information, so dig deep!

1. Brown University

   — — — — — — — — — — —

2. Navy War College

   — — — — — — —

3. Slater Mill

   — — — — — — — — — —

4. Old North Light Lighthouse

   — — — — — — — — — — —

5. Burlingame State Park

   — — — — — — — — — — — —

6. Gaspee Point

   — — — — — — — —

WORD BANK

Charlestown   Newport
Block Island   Providence
Charlestown   Pawtucket

ANSWERS: 1-Providence; 2-Newport; 3-Pawtucket; 4-Block Island; 5-Charlestown; 6-Warwick

Colonial Corn Husk Doll

You can make a corn husk doll similar to the dolls Rhode Island colonists' children played with! Here's how:

You will need:
- corn husks (or strips of cloth)
- string
- scissors

1. **Select a long piece of corn husk and fold it in half. Tie a string about one inch (2.54 centimeters) down from the fold to make the doll's head.**

2. **Roll a husk and put it between the layers of the tied husk, next to the string. Tie another string around the longer husk, just below the rolled husk. Now your doll has arms! Tie short pieces of string at the ends of the rolled husk to make the doll's hands.**

3. **Make your doll's waist by tying another string around the longer husk.**

4. **If you want your doll to have legs, cut the longer husk up the middle. Tie the two halves at the bottom to make feet.**

5. **Add eyes and a nose to your doll with a marker. You could use corn silk for the doll's hair.**

Now you can make a whole family of dolls!

©2001 Carole Marsh/Gallopade International/800-536-2GET/www.rhodeislandexperience.com/Page 68

Rhode Island Timeline!

A timeline is a list of important events and the year that they happened. You can use a timeline to understand more about history. **Read the timeline about Rhode Island history, then see if you can answer the questions at the bottom.**

1614	Dutch navigator Adriaen Block explores the coast
1636	Roger Williams arrives in what is now Rhode Island and founds Providence
1776	Rhode Island becomes first colony to renounce allegiance to England
1790	Rhode Island becomes the 13th state
1843	Rhode Island adopts new constitution after Dorr Rebellion
1883	U.S. Navy opens Newport Naval Station
1900	Providence becomes the official state capital
1935	State government reorganized in "Bloodless Revolution"
1938	Hurricane strikes Rhode Island, killing about 250 people and causing millions of dollars in property damage
1969	Newport Bridge from Jamestown to Newport dedicated
1973	Quonset Point Naval Air Station closed

Now put yourself back in the proper year if you were the following people.

1. You're a sailor on the ship commanded by Dutch navigator Adriaen Block, you may have spotted present-day Block Island in _____.

2. You suddenly reassigned to another Naval base since the Quonset Naval Air Station closes in _____.

3. You're upset with England for levying taxes on your shipping business and cheer when Rhode Island declares independence in _____.

4. A hurricane strikes the state in _____. Your home sustains flood damage.

5. You are a follower of Thomas Dorr and his People's party. In _____ you elected Dorr governor, the culmination of the Dorr rebellion.

6. The Newport Bridge is dedicated in _____, shortening your ride from Jamestown to Newport.

7. As a proud and patriotic Rhode Islander, you're thrilled to see your colony become a state in_____

8. You're a Congregationalist from Massachusetts in search of religious freedom. In _____ you settle in Providence.

ANSWERS: 1-1614; 2-1973; 3-1776; 4-1938; 5-1843; 6-1969; 7-1790; 8-1636

©2001 Carole Marsh/Gallopade International/800-536-2GET/www.rhodeislandexperience.com/Page 69

Rhode Island State Economy!

Rhode Island banks provide essential financial services.
Some of the services that banks provide include:
- They lend money to consumers to purchase goods and services such as houses, cars, and education.
- They lend money to producers who start new businesses.
- They issue credit cards.
- They provide savings accounts and pay interest to savers.
- They provide checking accounts.

Circle whether you would have more, less, or the same amount of money after each event.

1. You deposit your paycheck into your checking account.   MORE   LESS   SAME
2. You put $1,000 in your savings account.   MORE   LESS   SAME
3. You use your credit card to buy new school clothes.   MORE   LESS   SAME
4. You borrow money from the bank to open a toy store.   MORE   LESS   SAME
5. You write a check at the grocery store.   MORE   LESS   SAME
6. You transfer money from checking to savings.   MORE   LESS   SAME

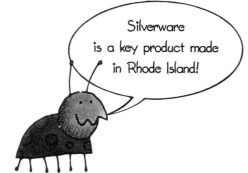

ANSWERS: 1. more 2. more 3. less 4. more 5. less 6. same

I Am A Famous Person From Rhode Island

From the Word Bank, find my name and fill in the blank.

WORD BANK
Esek Hopkins
Ambrose Burnside
Nathanael Greene
Ruth Ann Buzzi
Julia Ward Howe
H.P. Lovecraft

1. I was born near North Scituate and served as first commander-in-chief of the Continental navy.

   Who am I? _____ _____

2. I was a politician and soldier. My bushy cheek hair became known as "sideburns."

   Who am I? _____ _____

3. I was born in Warwick. As a military leader, I was second in command to General George Washington.

   Who am I? _____ _____

4. I'm a very funny lady who was born in Westerly. You can see me on *Sesame Street*.

   Who am I? _____ _____

5. I was a writer and poet. I am best known for writing the "Battle Hymn of the Republic."

   Who am I? _____ _____

6. I was born in Providence. My eerie novels and stories have supernatural characters.

   Who am I? _____ _____

ANSWERS: 1-Esek Hopkins; 2-Ambrose Burnside; 3-Nathanael Greene; 4-Ruth Ann Buzzi; 5-Julia Ward Howe; 6-H.P. Lovecraft

Artifacts Abound in Rhode Island!

According to archaeologists, there were about 10,000 Indians living in present-day Rhode Island. The majority belonged to the Narragansett tribe. In Charlestown, there is a 2,500-acre Narragansett Indian Reservation which was home to this tribe known as "the people of the small point." Nearby is the Royal Indian Burial ground. The early inhabitants were farmers and fishermen.

You are an archaeologist digging into one of the ancient settlement along the shorelines in Rhode Island. Below are pictures of some of the artifacts that you find. Now, you have to identify these strange objects and their uses. **Write down what you think these things are for!**

Rhode Island Native Americans!

When the settlers arrived in Rhode Island, there were several Native American groups already living there: The Narragansett, Wampanoag, Nipmuc, Niantic, and Pequot.

Draw a line from the group to its location on the map.

- The Narragansett was the largest and most powerful group. Narragansett occupied most of the area from present-day Providence, south to Narragansett Bay.

- The Wampanoag lived east of Narragansett Bay. The Nipmuc lived in the northern portion of Rhode Island and into Massachusetts and Connecticut.

- The Niantic occupied southwestern Rhode Island and coastal Connecticut.

- The Pequot had some land along the state's western border but lived mostly in Connecticut.

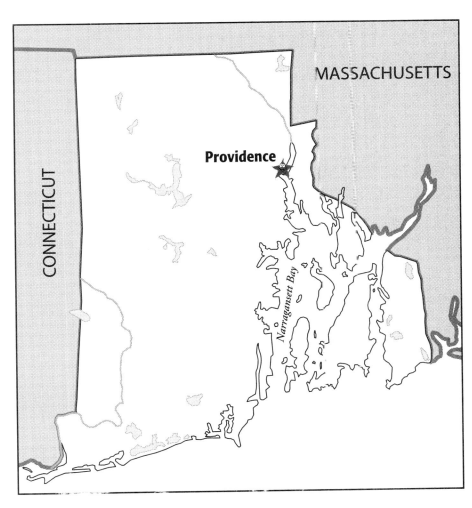

IT'S MONEY IN THE BANK!!

You spent the summer working at Gorham, a silver producing company, and you made a lot of money...$500 to be exact!
Solve the math problems below.

TOTAL EARNED: $500.00

I will pay back my Mom this much for money I borrowed when I first started working. Thanks, Mom!   A. $20.00

      subtract A from $500   B. _____

I will give my little brother this much money for taking my phone messages while I was at work: C. $10.00

      subtract C from B   D. _____

I will spend this much on a special treat or reward for myself: E. $25.00

      subtract E from D   F. _____

I will save this much for college: G. $300.00

      subtract G from F   H. _____

I will put this much in my new savings account so I can buy school clothes: I. $100.00

      subtract I from H   J. _____

TOTAL STILL AVAILABLE

                 (use answer J)   _____

TOTAL SPENT   (add A, C, and E)   _____

ANSWERS: B. $480; D. $470; F. $445; H. $145; J. $45; total available: $45; total spent: $55

Searching for Rhode Island Cities!

Find the following Rhode Island cities in the Word Search below.

WORD BANK

ARCTIC   BRISTOL   CHARLESTOWN

CRANSTON   NEWPORT   PAWTUCKET

PORTSMOUTH   PROVIDENCE   TIVERTON

WARWICK   WICKFORD   WOONSOCKET

```
C  I  H  J  X  U  C  N  I  E  J  T  Z  N  B
V  I  B  B  H  S  H  D  S  A  W  W  H  R  I
B  T  T  G  W  W  A  X  M  T  P  N  I  T  H
O  H  I  C  A  O  R  Z  O  S  S  I  E  Y
T  V  L  V  R  O  L  J  R  V  T  A  L  K  W
E  E  X  M  E  A  E  T  N  O  H  E  W  C  A
E  U  K  H  W  R  S  O  L  L  I  W  X  U  R
E  X  B  C  Q  M  T  R  O  P  W  E  N  T  W
C  V  K  O  O  S  O  O  S  F  T  E  E  W  I
C  J  S  U  N  S  W  S  N  O  K  W  X  A  C
D  J  T  A  E  C  N  E  D  I  V  O  R  P  K
Y  H  R  S  Q  H  E  O  I  A  P  G  N  P  Q
D  C  C  W  I  C  K  F  O  R  D  M  I  F  S
J  Y  Q  T  K  K  V  W  K  W  N  G  G  I  U
S  N  Z  B  M  P  X  Y  X  E  S  B  J  C  L
```

©2001 Carole Marsh/Gallopade International/800-536-2GET/www.rhodeislandexperience.com/Page 75

Numbering the Rhode Islanders!

STATE OF RHODE ISLAND
CENSUS REPORT

Every ten years, it's time for Rhode Islanders to stand up and be counted. Since 1790, the United States has conducted a census, or count, of each of its citizens. **Practice filling out a pretend census form.**

Name _____ Age ☐

Place of Birth _____

Current Address _____

Does your family own or rent where you live? _____

How long have you lived in Rhode Island? _____

How many people are in your family? _____

How many females? ☐   How many males? ☐

What are their ages? _____

How many rooms are in your house? ☐

How is your home heated? _____

How many cars does your family own? ☐

How many telephones are in your home? ☐

Is your home a farm? _____

Sounds pretty nosy, doesn't it? But a census is very important. The information is used for all kinds of purposes, including setting budgets, zoning land, determining how many schools to build, and much more. The census helps Rhode Island leaders plan for the future needs of its citizens. Hey, that's you!!

©2001 Carole Marsh/Gallopade International/800-536-2GET/www.rhodeislandexperience.com/Page 76

Endangered and Threatened Rhode Island!

Each state has a list of the endangered species found within its borders. An animal is labeled endangered when it is at risk of becoming extinct, or dying out completely. Land development, changes in climate and weather, and changes in the number of predators are all factors that can cause an animal to become extinct. Today many states are passing laws to help save animals on the endangered species list.

Can you help rescue these endangered and threatened animals by filling in their names below?

1. P _ _ _

2. _ _ U _ _ E _ N

3. _ H _ L _ S

4. T _ _ N _

5. _ _ A _ _ R _ _ E

Circle the animal that is extinct (not here anymore).

ANSWERS: 1-puma; 2-sturgeon; 3-whales; 4-terns; 5-sea turtle

©2001 Carole Marsh/Gallopade International/800-536-2GET/www.rhodeislandexperience.com/Page 77

Little Rhody...
A Great State and Song!

"Rhode Island" with words and music by T. Clarke Brown, was adopted as the state song in 1946.

> Here's to you, belov'd Rhode Island,
> With your Hills and Ocean Shore,
> We are proud to hail you "Rhody"
> And your Patriots of yore.
> First to claim your Independence,
> Rich your heritage and fame,
> The smallest State, smallest State
> and yet so great, so great
> We will glorify your name.

Answer the following questions:

1. What is a nickname for Rhode Island contained in the song?

   _____

2. Is Rhode Island the largest or smallest state in the union?

   _____

3. What two topographical features are mentioned in the song?

   _____

ANSWERS: 1-Rhody; 2-smallest; 3-hills, ocean shore

Getting Ready To Vote in Rhode Island

When you turn 18, you will be eligible to vote. Your vote counts! Many elections have been won by just a few votes. **The following is a form for your personal voting information. You will need to do some research to get all the answers!**

I will be eligible to vote on this date _____

I live in this Congressional District _____

I live in this State Senate District _____

I live in this State Representative District _____

I live in this Voting Precinct _____

The first local election I can vote in will be _____

The first state election I can vote in will be _____

The first national election I can vote in will be _____

The governor of our state is _____

One of my state senators is _____

One of my state representatives is _____

The local public office I would like to run for is _____

The state public office I would like to run for is _____

The federal public office I would like to run for is _____

Did you know that our state government has 50 senators?

The number of legislators may change after each census.

No, but I do know we have 100 representatives!

©2001 Carole Marsh/Gallopade International/800-536-2GET/www.rhodeislandexperience.com/Page 79

The Rhode Island State Seal

The state seal of Rhode Island features a golden anchor with the word "HOPE" inscribed above it. The border around the anchor says, "Seal of the State of Rhode Island Plantations 1636." The year commemorates Roger Williams' original settlement.

Color the state seal.

The anchor has been a symbol of Rhode Island since before it was a state!

The word "Hope" was placed over the anchor in 1644.

Rhode Island State Symbol Scramble!

Unscramble the names of these symbols for the state of Rhode Island. Write the answers in the word wheel around the picture of each symbol.

1. HRDEO SIDALN DRE HECICKN
   Hint: Rhode Island's state bird; developed on a farm in Little Compton in the 1850s
2. DRE AMPEL
   Rhode Island's state tree; an excellent shade tree with beautiful fall leaves
3. WOBNEITE
   Rhode Island's state mineral; a semiprecious gemstone that is similar to jade
4. TVOILE
   Rhode Island's state flower; grow wild in most parts of the world
5. GHQUOA
   Rhode Island's state shell; Narragansett Indians used it for food and for money

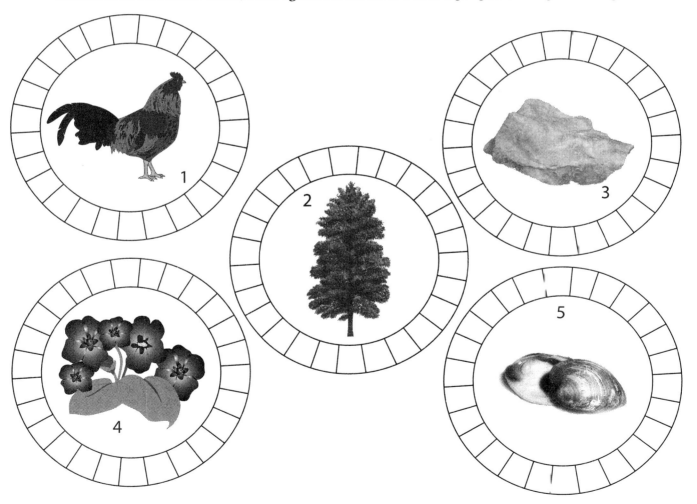

ANSWERS: 1-Red Chicken; 2-red maple; 3-bowenite; 4-violet; 5-quahog

©2001 Carole Marsh/Gallopade International/800-536-2GET/www.rhodeislandexperience.com/Page 81

A Quilt Of Many Counties

Rhode Island has five counties: Providence, Kent, Washington, Bristol, and Newport. There is no county government; instead, 39 municipalities cover the state and run the local governments.

- **Label your county. Color it red.**
- **Label the counties that neighbor your county. Color them blue.**
- **Now color the rest of the counties green.**

Contributions by Rhode Island Minorities!

Rhode Island is one of the most culturally diverse states in the union. Since its first settlements in the 1600s founded for freedom of religious expression, Rhode Island has been a haven for people from other American colonies and countries. As a result, minorities have made signficant contributions to the state.

Christiana Cartreax Bannister and Edward Bannister were a notable Providence couple who were influential in the arts and social causes. Christiana, who was part-black and part-Indian, established herself as a successful businesswoman in the 1850s through her hair salons. She hired Edward Bannister, an aspiring free black man and artist, to work as a barber in one of her shops in 1853. Four years later they married, and Edward quit cutting hair to develop his talent as a landscape and seascape painter. During the Civil War, Christiana was involved in the movement to pay black soldiers serving in the 4th Regiment equal pay and benefits. She was president of Boston's Sanitary Fair of Colored Ladies and held fundraisers to raise money for the wives and children of underpaid soldiers. Christiana was also influential in founding the Home for Aged Colored Women, the present day Bannister House. This was a place for homeless black domestic workers. She later moved into the home she helped to establish. She died there in 1902.

Fact or opinion?

1. Rhode Island was right to welcome people of other cultures and religions.

    _____

2. Christiana Cartreux Bannister was businesswoman and social reformer.

    _____

3. Edward Bannister was a free Black man and artist.

    _____

4. It was an outrage that black soldiers were underpaid during the Civil War.

    _____

5. Christiana Cartreux Bannister founded a home for aging Black domestic workers.

    _____

ANSWERS: 1-opinion; 2-fact; 3-fact; 4-opinion; 5-fact

Sub Attack!

It's a bird! It's a plane! No, it's a **submarine**! Visible in Narragansett Bay off Newport is the remains of a German U-853 submarine that went down in one of the final battles of World War II. Today, **observers** can see about 100 feet (30 meters) of the **vessel** protruding above the **surface** of the water.

Due to some **miscommunication** between the Germans about the end of the war in May 1945, the submarine was still on active duty when it **torpedoed** and sank an American vessel. The Americans returned fire and sank the submarine, or U-boat. The sub is **positioned** straight up and down in the surf.

See if you can figure out the meanings of these words from the story above.

submarine _____

_____

observers _____

_____

vessel _____

_____

protruding _____

_____

surface _____

_____

miscommunication _____

_____

torpedoed _____

_____

positioned _____

_____

Now check your answers in a dictionary. How close did you get to the real definitions?

Which Founding Person Am I?

From the Word Bank, find my name and fill in the blank.

WORD BANK
Adriaen Block
Ann and William Hutchinson
Giovanni da Verrazzano
Roger Williams
Samuel Gorton
William Blackstone

1. I was an Italian explorer who first sailed into present day Narragansett Bay in 1524.

   Who am I? _____

2. I was an Englishman who founded Providence as a haven for people seeking religious and political freedom in 1631.

   Who am I? _____

3. We settled Pocasset which is present-day Portsmouth.

   Who are we? _____

4. I discovered present-day Block Island in 1614.

   Who am I? _____

5. I am recognized as Rhode Island's first white settler.

   Who am I? _____

6. I founded the city of Warwick.

   Who am I? _____

ANSWERS: 1-Giovanni da Verrazzano; 2-Roger Williams; 3-Ann and William Hutchinson; 4-Adriaen Block; 5-William Blackstone

It Could Happen— And It Did!

These historical events from Rhode Island's past are all out of order. Can you put them back together in the correct order? Number these events from 1 to 10, beginning with the earliest. (There's a great big hint at the end of each sentence.)

_____ Williams receives charter for Rhode Island (1644)

_____ Giovanni da Verrazzano sails into present-day Narragansett Bay (1524)

_____ Rhode Island's general assembly outfits two war ships and forms the first U.S. Navy (1775)

_____ Rhode Island soldiers fire at British ships in Narragansett Bay, inciting one of first battles in the Revolutionary war (1764)

_____ U.S. Navy opens Newport Naval Station (1883)

_____ Rhode Island becomes the 13th state (1790)

_____ Rhode Island adopts new constitution after Dorr Rebellion (1843)

_____ Hurricane strikes Rhode Island, killing about 250 people and causing millions of dollars in property damage (1938)

_____ Newport Bridge from Jamestown to Newport dedicated (1969)

_____ Constitutional Convention adopts amendments including home rule for cities and towns (1951)

ANSWERS: 2; 1; 4; 3; 7; 5; 6; 8; 10; 9

"Little Rhody's" Not So Little Capitol!

The Rhode Island State House is located on top of a hill that overlooks the city of Providence. The New York firm of McKim, Mead, and White designed the State House in 1892, and it was constructed between the years of 1895 and 1904. The State House was built of white Georgia marble, and has the fourth largest self-supporting marble dome in the world! (The largest is the dome of St. Peter's Basilica in Vatican City.)

More than 300,000 cubic feet (8,495 cubic meters) of Georgia marble, 15,000,000 bricks, and 1,309 tons (1,178 metric tons) of iron floor beams were used to build the capitol. The building costs added up to $3,018,416.33, and if a similar building were constructed today it would cost more than $1 billion dollars! The State House is 333 feet (101.5 meters) long, 189 feet (57.6 meters) wide at the central rotunda (domed part), and 235 feet (71.6 meters) tall from the terrace to the tip of the Independent Man statue's spear at the top of the dome!

Here is a picture of a capitol building similar to the Rhode Island State House. Label its length, height, and width at the rotunda, in feet. Then, write how many bricks, and how much weight (in pounds) of iron floor beams were used to build the capitol.

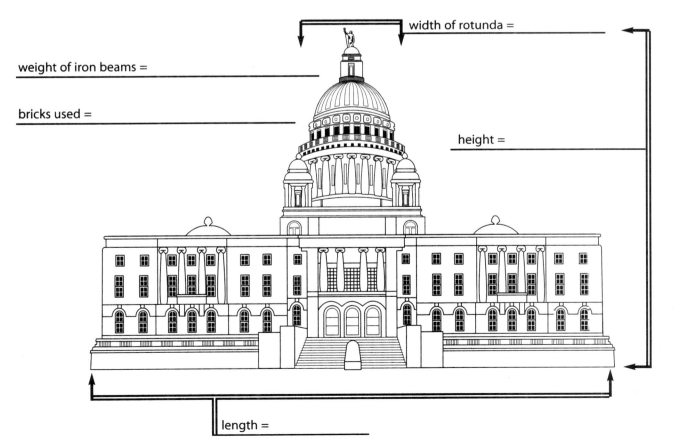

Rhode Island Word Wheel!

Using the Word Wheel of Rhode Island names, complete the sentences below.

1. Built in 1762, this building now houses the Rhode Island Heritage Commission and Historical Preservation Commission. _____

2. This was one of the first school buildings in the city: _____

3. The old state arsenal, designed by Russell Warren and built in 1839, is called _____.

4. This was the nation's first enclosed shopping mall, built in 1828 in Greek Revival style: _____

5. This was the first textile mill in the country powered by water: _____

6. At _____ Point, the Beavertail State Park preserves the original base of the third lighthouse established in America!

7. The _____ Farm in Jamestown is a 265-acre (107-hectare) working farm complete with animals, a large garden, and a 2-mile (3.2-kilometer) walking trail.

8. The _____ _____ Memorial Building in Jamestown includes a horse-drawn 1894 steam engine and other antique fire-fighting equipment.

9. _____ _____ and Arboretum in Bristol overlooks Narragansett Bay.

10. The _____ in Newport was built for Cornelius Vanderbuilt.

ANSWERS: 1-Old State House; 2-Brick School House; 3-Gothic Castle; 4-Providence Arcade; 5-Slater's Mill; 6-Beavertail; 7-Watson; 8-Fire Department; 9-Blithewold Gardens; 10-Breakers

Rhode Island Pop Quiz!

Pop quiz! It's time to test your knowledge of Rhode Island! Try to answer all of the questions before you look at the answers.

1. What is the capital of Rhode Island?
   a. Providence
   b. Pawtucket
   c. Cranston

2. Where did the American Industrial Revolution begin?
   a. Rhode Island
   b. Massachusetts
   c. Connecticut

3. This was a popular site for wealthy New Yorkers to vacation at the turn of the 20th century.
   a. Newport
   b. Bristol
   c. Jamestown

4. Which family was influential and contributed to the educational and economic development of Rhode Island?
   a. Greens
   b. Browns
   c. Blacks

5. What is Rhode Island's state motto?
   a. Be Free
   b. Hope
   c. Discover

6. What is Rhode Island's official nickname?
   a. Scenic State
   b. Rich State
   c. Ocean State

7. Which senator, from Rhode Island, was one of the U.S. Senate's longest serving members?
   a. Strom Thurmond
   b. Theodore Green
   c. William Blackstone

8. Which tribe was the largest among Native American tribes in Rhode Island.
   a. Cherokee
   b. Lenni Lenape
   c. Narragansett

9. This branch of the armed services has its roots in Rhode Island.
   a. Army
   b. Marines
   c. Navy

10. What is a quahog?
    a. clam
    b. shrimp
    c. mussel

ANSWERS: 1-a; 2-a; 3-a; 4-b; 5-b; 6-c; 7-b; 8-c; 9-c; 10-a

Tennis, Anyone?

Yacht racing and tennis are probably the first sports that come to mind when you think of Rhode Island. Newport was the site of America's Cup races for more than 30 years and still hosts the Newport to Bermuda Races and several other prestigious events. Weekend sailing enthusiasts regularly hoist their sails for club-sponsored regattas. Tennis, played on grass courts, was an activity enjoyed by the wealthy summer residents of Newport during its Gilded Age. Today, the courts are still in use at the Newport Casino, International Tennis Hall of Fame.

In each pair of sentences below, one of the statements is false. Read them carefully and choose the sentence that is not true. Cross out the false sentence, and circle the true sentence.

1. Sailing is a popular sport in Rhode Island.
   Sailing is no longer a popular sport in Rhode Island.

2. Tennis cannot be played on grass courts.
   Tennis can be played on grass and clay courts.

3. Newport is home to the International Tennis Hall of Fame.
   Bermuda is home to International Tennis Hall of Fame.

4. The Gilded Age in Newport was a time of sport and lavish entertaining.
   The Gilded Age was a difficult time for Rhode Islanders.

5. Many of Rhode Island's sports activities take place on water.
   Many of Rhode Island's sports are land-based.

ANSWERS: Sentences which are true: 1-first; 2-second; 3-first; 4-first; 5-first

The Rhode Island Lights!

Because Rhode Island has about 400 miles (644 kilometers) of coastline, many lighthouses were constructed to help guide ships to their ports. Today, more than 10 of those lighthouses are still functioning. Most are not open to the public. The Watch Hill Light on Fishers Island, which includes a lighthouse history museum, was first built in 1808. It is still operational, and has a tower that is 45 feet (13.7 meters) tall. The North Block Island light, which also has a museum, was established in 1829, and its tower stands 55 feet (16.8 meters). The Castle Hill Lighthouse in Newport, established in 1890 and home to a Coast Guard station, has a 34-foot (10.4-meter) tall tower. The Conimicut Shoal Light at the mouth of the Providence River has a 58-foot (17.7-meter) tall tower, and was established in 1868.

Using the information in the paragraphs above, graph the heights, in feet, of the different lighthouses listed. The first one has been done for you.

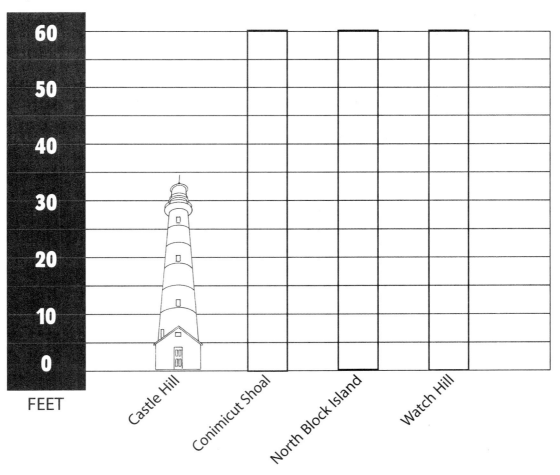

Quoth the Quahog, "I'm the State Shell!"

In 1987, Rhode Island adopted its official state shell. Kay Peterson, a conchologist (person who studies seashells and the animals living in them) asked the Coventry, Rhode Island, Junior High School Shell Club if they could think of the perfect shell. The quahog, a hard-shelled clam whose shells were used as wampum by the Native Americans, was chosen.

The quahog (its Latin name is *Mercenaria mercenaria*) is usually found just below the sand or mud surface of Narragansett Bay. Quahogs with a one-inch (2.5-centimeter) to 2.5-inch (6.4-centimeter) thick shell are called littlenecks. Quahogs with 2.5-inch (6.5-centimeter) to 3-inch (7.5-centimeter) thick shells are called cherrystones. Chowders are quahogs with shells thicker than 3 inches (7.5-centimeter). Rhode Island is right in the middle of "quahog country," and since 1980 has supplied one-fourth of the nation's total annual commercial quahog catch each year!

A *haiku* is a three-line poem with a certain number of syllables in each line. Look at the example below:

The first line has 5 syllables:	Lit/tle qua/hog shell,
The second line has 7 syllables:	Lit/tle/necks, cher/ry/stones, all,
The third line has 5 syllables:	You, quite a state shell!

Now write your own *haiku* about the quintessential quahog!

Sail Away to Rhode Island!

The Continental sloop *Providence* is a 110-foot (34-meter) sailing vessel moored in Narragansett Bay. The full-rigged ship is a replica of the *Providence* under Captain John Paul Jones' command in the War of Independence. During the vessel's tour of duty, she sank or captured 40 British enemy ships with her twelve guns.

See if you can label the parts of the sailing sloop below. Use the following definitions to help you!

mast-a tall pole near the center of the ship
stern-the rear portion of the ship
deck-Top surface of the ship where sailors may stand
bow-the pointed front of the ship
sails-the billowing white sheets that fill with air
rudder-the shaped steering piece on the rear of the ship
keel-shaped, weighted plate, which steadies the ship below the water

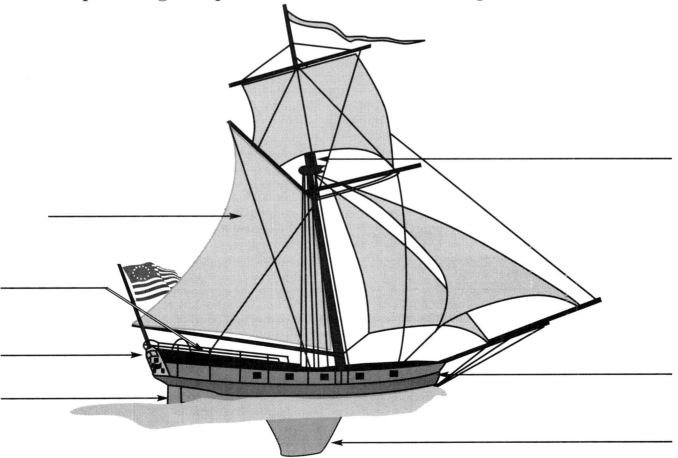

How Big is Rhode Island?

Rhode Island is the smallest state in the United States! It has an area of approximately 1,231 square miles (1,981 square kilometers).

Can you answer the following questions?

1. How many states are there in the United States?
   _____

2. This many states are smaller than our state:
   _____

3. This many states are larger than our state:
   _____

4. One mile = 5,280 ____ ____ ____ ____

   HINT:

5. Draw a square foot.

6. Classroom Challenge: After you have drawn a square foot, measure the number of square feet in your classroom. Most floor tiles are square feet (12 inches by 12 inches). How many square feet are in your classroom? _____

Bonus: Try to calculate how many classrooms would fit in the total area of your state. _____

Hint: About 46,464 average classrooms would fit in just one square mile!

ANSWERS: 1-50; 2-0; 3-49; 4-feet; 5-answers will vary; 6-answers will vary
BONUS: 57,197,184 classrooms!

©2001 Carole Marsh/Gallopade International/800-536-2GET/www.rhodeislandexperience.com/Page 94

The Browns of Rhode Island!

One of the most important and influential families in the New England colonies was a Rhode Islander clan by the name of Brown. Four of the Brown brothers helped to make history. Nicholas, John, Moses, and Joseph were heavily involved in Rhode Island's development. Nicholas and John were merchants, and John sent merchant ships to Africa, Europe, Asia, and the Caribbean Islands. Nicholas Brown also gave major support to Rhode Island College (which was later renamed for his family). Joseph was an architect, and designed many of the buildings in Providence. Moses was an industrialist who helped to establish the first cotton mills in Rhode Island. Moses was also an abolitionist who actually opposed his brother John's involvement in the slave trade. Moses co-founded the Providence Society for Abolishing the Slave Trade.

Answer the following questions about the Brown brothers.

1. Which Brown was an abolitionist?

   _____

2. Which Brown designed several Providence buildings?

   _____

3. Which Brown supported Rhode Island College?

   _____

4. Which Browns were merchants?

   _____

5. Which Brown helped to establish the first cotton mills?

   _____

ANSWERS: 1-Moses; 2-Joseph; 3-Nicholas; 4-John and Nicholas; 5-Moses

Acrostically Speaking in Rhode Island....

The words below are known as an acrostic. See if you can make up your own acrostic poem describing Rhode Island. For each letter in Rhode Island's name, write down a word or phrase that describes Rhode Island. The first is done for you.

R is for REVOLUTIONARY